Away With Words

The Daring Story of Isabella Bird

Written by **Lori Mortensen**

Illustrated by **Kristy Caldwell**

PEACHTREE
ATLANTA

To my daring family, and the exquisite books that
regularly take me away with their words.
—L. M.

For Rachael, Kim, and Marshall
—K. C.

Ω

Published by
Peachtree Publishers
1700 Chattahoochee Avenue
Atlanta, Georgia 30318-2112
www.peachtree-online.com

Text © 2019 by Lori Mortensen
Illustrations © 2019 by Kristy Caldwell

Edited by Kathy Landwehr
Design and composition by Nicola Simmonds Carmack

The illustrations were rendered digitally.

Printed in October 2018 by Tien Wah Press in Malaysia
10 9 8 7 6 5 4 3 2 1
First Edition
ISBN 978-1-68263-005-1

Library of Congress Cataloging-in-Publication Data

Names: Mortensen, Lori, 1955– author. | Caldwell, Kristy, illustrator.
Title: Away with words : the daring story of Isabella Bird / written by Lori
Mortensen ; illustrated by Kristy Caldwell.
Description: Atlanta : Peachtree Publishers, [2019]
Identifiers: LCCN 2017018780 | ISBN 9781682630051
Subjects: LCSH: Bird, Isabella L. (Isabella Lucy), 1831–1904—Juvenile literature. |
Women travelers—Great Britain—Biography—Juvenile literature.
Classification: LCC G246.B5 M67 2019 | DDC 910.4092 [B] — dc23 LC record
available at *https://lccn.loc.gov/2017018780*

Isabella Bird was like a wild vine
stuck in a too-small pot.
She needed more room.
She had to get out.
She had to explore.

But petite Isabella,
pale Isabella,
proper Isabella
was an unlikely candidate for adventure.

Born in 1831, Isabella had suffered from mysterious aches and pains ever since she was small. While her little sister Hennie scampered about their sturdy home nestled in the English countryside, Isabella rested.

I very tired.

Poor dear!
What can be done?

No one knew how to help her.
Would Isabella simply wilt away?

Isabella's family took her to a number of doctors, but none of them could figure out what was wrong.

Then, one day a doctor made a suggestion. Maybe she needed fresh air.

Her father set Isabella upon his horse. Together, they visited his parishioners in the wide open air of the English countryside. As they clippety-clopped along, he drew her attention to every feature in the wayside and questioned her about them.

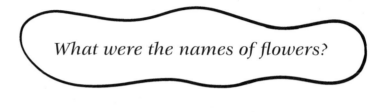

What were the names of flowers?

roses...lilies...saxifrages...

What were the names of the animals?

hares...sheep...foxes...starlings...

What were the names of the crops?

rye...wheat...barley...

With each question asked, young Isabella learned more.

Out in the wild, Isabella forgot about her aches and pains. She breathed in new ways to see and describe everything around her.

Question by question, word by word, Isabella bloomed.

As she grew, Isabella heard letters from her uncles in India and news from missions in Africa. She marveled at their descriptions of exotic sights.

giant elephants, colorful saris, curious monkeys, and twisted turbans

pungent smells... curry, orchids, incense and smoke

and soaring temperatures... 90...100...110!

Her head spun with the thrilling possibilities.

What faraway places would she explore?

What stunning details would fill *her* letters?

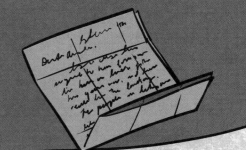

But as Isabella grew into a young lady, her wild-
vine world closed around her, small and snug.

Young ladies wore dresses.

Young ladies didn't go to school.

Young ladies stayed home.

Her life seemed over before it had even begun.

Some days, Isabella felt so low that she couldn't
even stir from the couch.

Slowly, Isabella wilted.

Aches and pains returned.

What could be done?

In time, her doctor made another suggestion. Maybe another change of air—this time, a sea voyage.

Isabella's heart quavered. It was a fortuitous twist of fate.

At twenty-two, Isabella pulled up roots. She packed her proper Victorian clothes and a red leather notebook, and climbed aboard a mail steamer bound for Nova Scotia.

Isabella sailed away.

Away from England.

Away from family.

And away from what a young

Englishwoman could and couldn't do.

Out in the wide world, Isabella soaked up each feature, just as she had atop her father's horse. She filled notebooks with stunning details. Nothing escaped her questioning gaze.

In America, Isabella rode trains *on narrow rims of metal* through dense forests and rolling prairies. She saw...

...he steamed down the mighty Mississippi and mingled ...ith traders, trappers, leathered prairie men *armed to ...e teeth,* and diggers on their way to find gold.

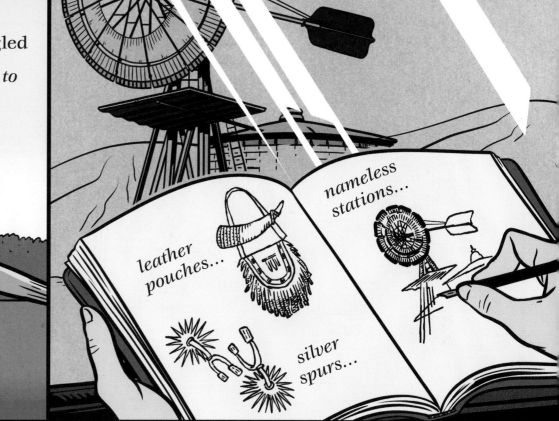

leather
pouches...

nameless
stations...

silver
spurs...

In this new land, it seemed as if everyone
lived as *free as the winds.*
For the first time, so did Isabella.

Two months later, Isabella returned home. She captivated family and friends with her remarkable tales. Her father encouraged her to write a book.

A book?

A book!

Armed with her notebook brimming with details of all she'd encountered—from foiling a pickpocket to withstanding the deafening roar of Niagara Falls—Isabella wrote *The Englishwoman in America*. It was published in 1856.

Isabella's vibrant descriptions made readers feel as if they'd explored rough-and-tumble America too.

Evening succeeded noon, and twilight to the blaze of a summer day; the yellow sun sank cloudless behind the waves of the rolling prairie...

There was a small bed with a dirty buffalo-skin upon it; I took it up and swarms of living creatures fell out of it...

Water is a beverage which I never enjoyed in purity and perfection before I visited America.

Enthralled with her new life, Isabella made
a second voyage to write a second book.
When she returned a year later in 1858, she
hoped for a joyful reunion with her family.
But that very night, her father fell ill.

One month later,
he was dead.

Suddenly, exploring the world seemed wrong. A proper woman stayed home. A proper woman sacrificed and set her own needs aside. A proper woman concerned herself with family.

Isabella reached a stunning conclusion. She had failed her duty and her father.

At twenty-six, wild-vine Isabella made a hard decision—as hard as the narrow rims of metal she had described in her book.

She would stop exploring.

She would be the dutiful daughter she was supposed to be.

Isabella moved with her mother and sister to a tidy house across from a church.

Mornings, she wrote.

Afternoons, she called on friends.

In time, Isabella's backaches, headaches, and sleepless nights returned yet again.

Month by month, year by year, Isabella held to her vow and sank into despair.

Finally, Hennie pleaded for her to follow her dreams.

Isabella reluctantly agreed.

In the summer of 1872, Isabella boarded a steamer in Liverpool bound for Australia. She was thirty-nine years old. Youth had passed, but the spirit of adventure still burned brightly.

Isabella abandoned her too-small pot once and for all.

Henceforth, she proclaimed, *I must live my own life.*

Isabella rode *spider-legged* horses,

muddy mules,

belligerent
camels,

and wide, willful elephants across five continents.

She wrote nine more astonishing books about her travels—all bestsellers!

Along each hard-won mile, she wrote in her journal, sketched pictures, and kept careful records.

How far she traveled.

The measure of the land.

The people she met.

Each voyage tested her mettle. Each place revealed something new.

In the Sandwich Islands, Isabella traded her skirt for bloomerlike *full Turkish trousers* and clambered up Kilauea, a towering, lava-spewing volcano. Up until then, she'd always worn a skirt and ridden sidesaddle—the ladylike way to ride. But concessions had to be made to climb a volcano.

Suddenly...gory drops were tossed in the air... It was all confusion, commotion, force, terror, glory, majesty, mystery, and even beauty.

In Persia, Isabella and her guides nearly froze riding across the numbing, windswept desert at *the roof of the world.*

The *demon wind seized on us...*, she wrote, *a steady, blighting, searching, merciless blast* that cut through her six layers of woolen clothing as if they were nothing.

Isabella admitted, *I was so helpless, and in such torture, that I would gladly have lain down to die in the snow.*

But Isabella pressed on and learned she could survive.

No matter where she went, she wondered.

Who would she meet?

What would she see?

How would she get there?

Isabella never knew.

That was part of the adventure.

In Colorado, she befriended Rocky Mountain Jim, a notorious outlaw, and climbed up Longs Peak, a daunting 14,000-foot mountain in the Rockies. *I had various falls,* she wrote, *and once hung by my frock, which caught on a rock, and "Jim" severed it with his hunting knife, upon which I fell into a crevice full of soft snow.*

In Malaysia, Isabella dined on curry, chutney, pineapple, eggs, and bananas with a friend's two pet apes

What a grotesque dinner party, she wrote. *What a delightful one!*

In Tibet, Isabella hiked for three grueling days until she reached a monastery built high in the snowcapped peaks.

Sharbaz! (Well done!) shouted the crowd.

An orchestra of blaring horns, thundering drums, and clashing cymbals echoed through the mountains, celebrating her arrival.

The *tornado of sound* nearly overwhelmed her. *It was not music,* she declared, *but it was sublime.*

But not everyone was welcoming.

In one Chinese village, an angry mob, suspicious of strangers, surrounded her, shouting:

Foreign devil!

Child-eater!

When they walloped her with sticks and mud, Isabella fled into a nearby inn's *dark and ruinous* lumber room.

The mob followed and tossed flaming matches onto the straw-covered floor.

Isabella handily snuffed them out, then waited, pistol in hand, until soldiers broke up the riotous crowd.

Leave?

Surrender?

Isabella remained undaunted.

Nothing—frostbite, cholera, broken bones, volcanic burns, attacks, and several near drownings—could quench her thirst to explore the unknown.

As word of her explorations grew, Isabella lectured to vast audiences. Her presentations were as spirited as her adventures.

People marveled that a woman had done such thing

Some people thought she'd gone too far for a proper lady.

In 1892, London's Royal Geographic Society honored Isabella. She became their first female member.

The following year, Isabella was presented to the Queen.

I am very much pleased to see you here, Mrs. Bishop.

For Her Majesty Queen Victoria

Young ladies wore dresses, but Isabella clothed herself with daring determination.

Young ladies didn't go to school, but Isabella's explorations enlightened the world.

Young ladies stayed home,

but to wild-vine Isabella...

...the world was home.

Author's Note

Isabella Bird grew up during the Victorian Age. Although her parents taught her French, literature, history, art, scriptures, Latin, and botany at home, society offered little opportunity for her or any other women of the era. The longer Isabella remained at home, the more depressed she became and the worse her symptoms grew. Once she sailed away from England, her spirit soared.

Traveling in earnest at middle age, Isabella explored unbeaten paths in Australia, New Zealand, The Sandwich Islands (Hawaii), the Rocky Mountains, Japan, India, Persia (Iran), Turkey, Korea, China, and Tibet. When she completed an adventure, she returned to England and wrote a book about it. After it was published, she set out on her next adventure. Some of her accounts became major news stories.

Although elements of English society troubled her, she remained faithful to her religious roots and performed good works throughout her life, training as a nurse and establishing several orphanages and missionary hospitals in Asia.

In 1881, fifty-year-old Isabella married John Bishop, a doctor and old family friend, and turned her attention to marriage. Just short of their fifth anniversary, Dr. Bishop passed away after a long illness. Isabella resumed traveling and continued to do so for the rest of her life.

While she still suffered from back pain, she found life far worse reposed on a Victorian sofa than forging new paths in distant lands. "No man," she once declared, "now ever says of any difficult thing that I could not do it!"

In 1882, Isabella studied photography and eagerly added this new tool to document her explorations. Although it was difficult to pack the big, bulky equipment on her journeys, meeting its unique demands along the rough and tumble miles was "a joy and a triumph." In China, she created a makeshift darkroom by stuffing blankets and newspapers into the cracks of her cabin. After developing and printing her negatives, she stretched over the gunwale of her boat and rinsed them in the wash of the Great River.

In 1901, Isabella sailed to Morocco in North Africa. After riding 500 miles astride a spirited black stallion through the Atlas Mountains, her health finally failed. She returned to England to recuperate. It was her final journey.

She was seventy years old.

On October 7, 1904, Isabella Lucy Bird Bishop died in Edinburgh. The *New York Times* declared she was "one of the most daring women travelers who ever lived."

A Timeline of Isabella Bird's Travels and Publications

1854
Canada and the United States

1856
An Englishwoman in America, her first book

1857–1858
Second trip to the United States

1859
The Aspects of Religion in the United States of America

1869
Notes on Old Edinburgh

1871
New York and the Mediterranean

1872–1873
Australia, New Zealand, Sandwich Islands (Hawaii), and the Rocky Mountains in the United States

1875
The Hawaiian Archipelago: Six Months among the Palm Groves, Coral Reefs and Volcanoes of the Sandwich Islands

1878–1879
Japan, the Malay Peninsula, and Egypt

1879
A Lady's Life in the Rocky Mountains

1880
Unbeaten Tracks in Japan: Six Months Among the Palm Groves, Coral Reefs and Volcanoes of the Sandwich Islands

1883
The Golden Chersonese and the Way Thither

February 1889
India, Tibet, Persia (Iran), Kurdistan, and Turkey
Founds John Bishop Memorial Hospital and Henrietta Bird Hospital for Women, both in India

1890
Becomes a Fellow of the Royal Scottish Geographical Society, the first woman to do so

1891
Journeys in Persia and Kurdistan

1892
Becomes a Fellow of the Royal Geographical Society, the first woman to do so

1893
Presented to Queen Victoria

1894
Among the Tibetans

1894–1897
Canada, Japan, Korea, and China
Founds one hospital in Korea and two in China, and an orphanage in Japan

1897
Elected to membership of the Royal Photographic Society

1898
Korea and Her Neighbours

1899
The Yangtze Valley and Beyond

1900
Morocco
Chinese Pictures: notes on photographs made in China

Many of Isabella Bird's books are available to read online for free.
Quotations in the text are from the following sources:

14
"on narrow rims of metal"
The Englishwoman in America, page 143

15
"armed to the teeth"
The Englishwoman in America, page 140

"free as the winds"
The Englishwoman in America, page 141

17
"Evening succeeded..."
The Englishwoman in America, page 143

"There was a small bed..."
The Englishwoman in America, page 148

"Water is a beverage..."
The Englishwoman in America, page 152

22
"Henceforth, I must..."
The Life of Isabella Bird (Mrs. Bishop), page 177

"spider-legged"
Among the Tibetans, page 72

24
"full Turkish trousers"
A Lady's Life in the Rocky Mountains, page vii

"Suddenly...gory drops..."
Six Months in the Sandwich Islands, page 83

25
"the roof of the world."
Journeys in Persia and Kurdistan, page 127

"demon wind..."
Journeys in Persia and Kurdistan, page 128

"I was so helpless..."
Journeys in Persia and Kurdistan, page 129

26
"I had various falls..."
A Lady's Life in the Rocky Mountains, page 115

27
"What a grotesque..."
The Golden Chersonese and the Way Thither, page 391

"tornado of sound"
Among the Tibetans, page 85

"It was not music..."
Among the Tibetans, page 85

28
"dark and ruinous"
Journeys in Persia and Kurdistan, page 52

30
"She...exercises..."
The Life of Isabella Bird (Mrs. Bishop), page 177

"No one has an adventure..."
The Spectator magazine, in their review of *A Lady's Life in the Rocky Mountains*

"the woman must be devoid..."
Sir Austen Henry Layard, quoted in *The Daily Mail*

31
"I am very much pleased..."
The Life of Isabella Bird (Mrs. Bishop), page 267

36
"No man..."
Letters to Henrietta, written by Isabella Bird and edited by Kay Chubbuck. Boston: Northeastern University Press, 2003.

Bibliography

Bird, Isabella Lucy. *The Englishwoman in America*. Toronto: University of Toronto Press, 1856.

Birkett, Dea. *Spinsters Traveling Abroad: Lady Victoria Explorers*. New York: Basil Blackwell, Inc., 1989.

Danneberg, Julie. *Amidst the Gold Dust: Women Who Forged the West*. Golden, Colorado: Fulcrum Publishing, 2001.

De Porti, Andrea. *Explorers: The Most Exciting Voyages of Discovery—from the Africa Expedition to the Lunar Landing.* Ontario: Firefly Books, 2005.

Halkon, Ruth. "Life of a Victorian adventuress: Incredible story of clergyman's daughter who braved malaria, floods and wars to trek across China" from the *Daily Mail* (*www.dailymail.co.uk/travel/travel_news/article-2999096/How-Victorian-adventuress-Isabella-Bird-braved-wars-survived-malaria-ignored-scorn-countrymen-best-selling-travel-writer-photojournalist.html*). March 18, 2015.

Havely, Cicely Palser, ed. *This Grand Beyond: The Travels of Isabella Bird Bishop*, London: Century Publishing, 1984.

Heaver, Stuart. "Isabella Bird, Victorian Pioneer Who Changed West's View of China" from *Post Magazine* (*www.scmp.com/magazines/post-magazine/article/1846990/isabella-bird-victorian-pioneer-who-changed-wests-view-china*). August 8, 2015.

Kaye, Evelyn. *Amazing Traveler Isabella Bird*. Boulder: Blue Panda Publications, 1999.

Lundy, Iain. "In the Footsteps of Isabella Bird," from *The Scotsman* (*www.scotsman.com/lifestyle/in-the-footsteps-of-isabella-bird-1-465989*). November 8, 2005.

Stoddart, Anna M. *The Life of Isabella Bird (Mrs. Bishop)*. London: John Murray, 1906. Retrieved from *www.archive.org/stream/lifeofisabellabi00stoduoft/lifeofisabellabi00stoduoft_djvu.txt*.

Walker, Ronald. *The Extraordinary Isabella Bird*, leaflet for Boroughbridge and District Historical Society.

"History, Biography, Voyages and Travel," from *The Westminster Review*, Volume 65 January–April 1856. New York: Leonard Scott & Co., 1856. page 341 Retrieved from *books.google.com/books?id=7Y3jvaDuPMC&pg=PA341&lpg=PA341&dq=the+englishwoman+in+america+review+1856&source=bl&ots=hDrYCtR9or&sig=KTTtdulYAep1vndVB3dpI5e7tSk&hl=en&sa=X&ved=0CCUQ6AEwAjgKahUKEwiup7nW46TIAhWCSIgKHWzkABA#v=onepage&q=the%20englishwoman%20in%20america%20review%201856&f=false*.

"Isabella Lucy Bird," from Tattenhall and District Local History, *www.tattenhallhistory.co.uk/isabella-lucy-bird*.

"Photograph album of Isabella Bird's travels on horseback from Baghdad to Tehran in 1890, 1890" from Online Archive of California, *www.oac.cdlib.org/findaid/ark:/13030/c8hh6m93*.

"Travels with Isabella Bird," from the National Library of Scotland (*www.nls.uk/about-us/films-made-by-nls/isabella-bird-transcript*). July 2009.

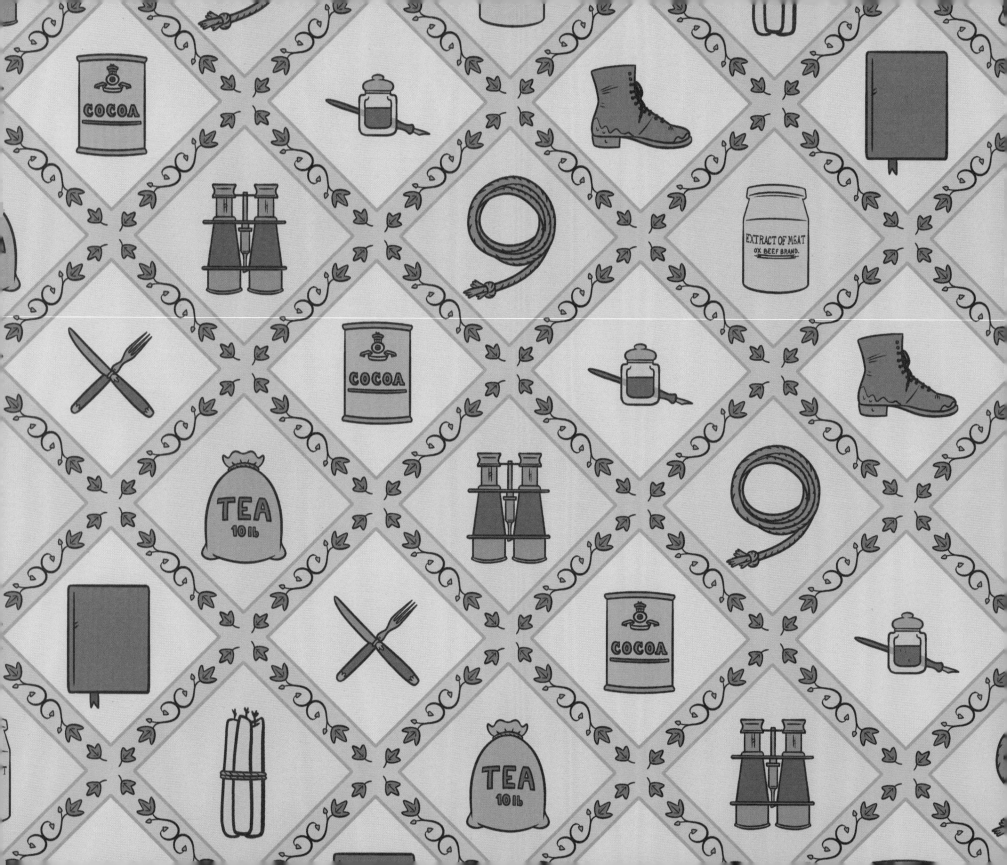